Bala Kids
An imprint of Shambhala Publications, Inc.
2129 13th Street
Boulder, Colorado 80302
www.shambhala.com

9 8 7 6 5 4 3 2 1

First Edition
Printed in China

♾ This edition is printed on acid-free paper that meets the American National Standards
Institute Z39.48 Standard.
♲ Shambhala makes every effort to print on postconsumer recycled paper. For more
information please visit www.shambhala.com.
Bala Kids is distributed worldwide by Penguin Random House, Inc., and its subsidiaries.

Designed by Kara Plikaitis

Library of Congress Cataloging-in-Publication Data
Names: Kanjuro, Carolyn, author. | Zohra, Sonali, illustrator.
Title: Ashoka the fierce: how an angry prince became India's emperor of peace / Carolyn
Kanjuro; illustrated by Sonali Zohra.
Description: First edition. | Boulder, Colorado: Bala Kids, An imprint of
Shambhala Publications, Inc., 2021 | Audience: Ages 6–10
Identifiers: LCCN 2020018724 | ISBN 9781611808544 (hardcover)
Subjects: LCSH: Aśoka, King of Magadha, active 259 B.C.–Juvenile
literature. | India–Kings and rulers–Biography–Juvenile literature. |
India–History–Maurya dynasty, ca. 322 B.C.–ca. 185 B.C.–Juvenile
literature. | Altruism–Juvenile literature. |
Buddhists–India–Biography–Juvenile literature.
Classification: LCC DS451.5 .K28 2021 | DDC 934/.045–dc23
LC record available at https://lccn.loc.gov/2020018724

ASHOKA the FIERCE

How an Angry Prince Became India's Emperor of Peace

ILLUSTRATED BY

Carolyn Kanjuro   Sonali Zohra

bala kids

Prince Ashoka was born all wrong. As the son of a great emperor, he should have been tall and muscular, with smooth skin the color of sandalwood. And he ought to have had the easy, charming confidence of a ruler-to-be. But the young prince was none of these things. He was short and pudgy, and his skin was covered in rough, dark patches that itched all the time. Worst of all, he could not control his temper.

His father made no secret of his disappointment in his son and gave all his attention to Ashoka's older brother Susima, who seemed to have everything Ashoka didn't.

"I don't care!" Ashoka would yell when his brothers poked fun at him. And he'd kick the dirt or throw a rock at whoever crossed him.

"That child is fierce," people whispered (for one didn't dare speak loudly against a son of the emperor). Over time he became known as Ashoka the Fierce.

Ashoka longed to gain the love and respect of his father, so he worked hard to excel in his studies–geography, history, horsemanship, and combat techniques. But his efforts did not sway his father's affections, and they didn't stop the other children from teasing him.

Over time, a cold, dark hole settled into Ashoka's heart where the light of his father's love should have shone. As he grew into a young man, he learned to fight for what he needed and to need very little from others.

"Your son Ashoka is showing remarkable skill, Your Majesty."

The emperor and his minister, Radhagupta, looked out over the training field as Ashoka and Susima competed with their bows and arrows. Distracted by friends cheering him on, Susima missed the mark. Ashoka shot straight through.

"It appears he might be well suited for leadership," the minister continued.

The emperor turned away from the window. "A boy like that cannot lead our great empire."

Sometimes even an emperor cannot see clearly, thought the minister.

Years passed, and the king fell ill. As he lay dying, he announced
the successor to his throne: Susima.

"*You* must be king," Radhagupta told Ashoka immediately after
the king passed.

"I cannot go against my father's will," he protested, though the
words tasted bitter in his mouth.

"Do not be shortsighted like your father," said the minister.
"Our realm needs a ruler with great vision and strength—and one
who knows how to listen to his advisers. We will back you."

So it came to pass that Ashoka defeated his brother Susima for the crown with the help of the powerful ministers. Some stories say Ashoka tricked his brother into falling into a pit of hot coals. Others say he killed six of his brothers vying for the crown; even taller tales say he killed ninety-nine brothers. The truth is, we do not know exactly how it happened–only that the skilled, rough-skinned boy grew to rule the Mauryan Empire.

In the first years of his reign, Ashoka ran the empire much as his father had, and his father's father before him. The realm remained stable under his rule, but he felt like little more than a manager of his father's vast domain.

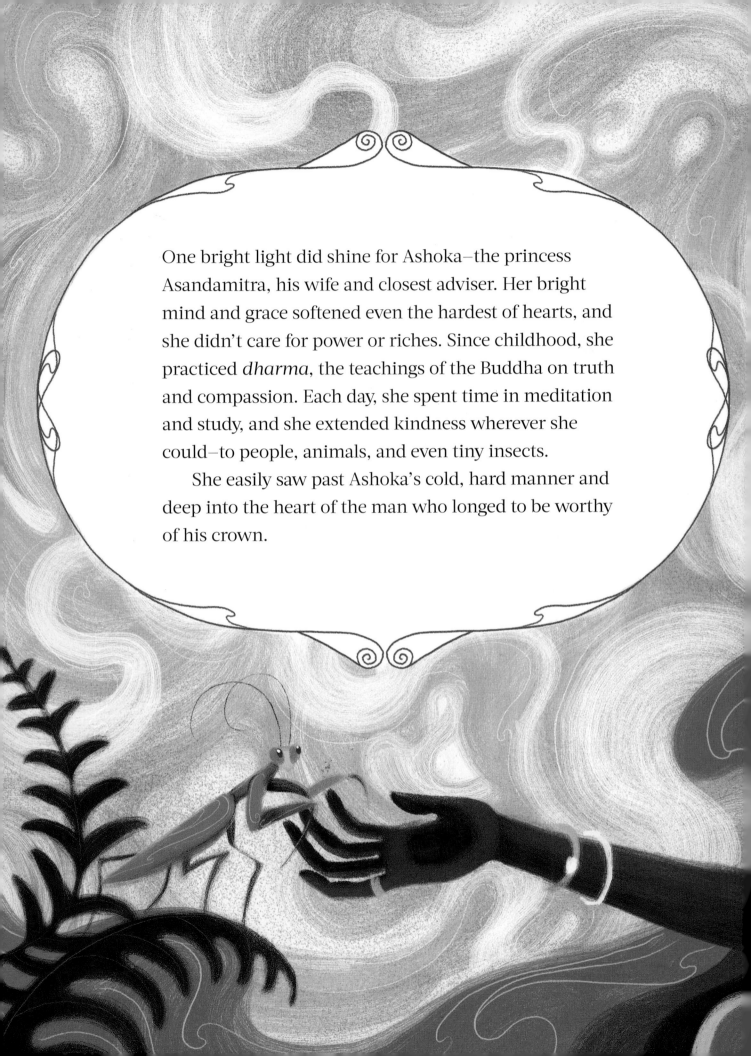

One bright light did shine for Ashoka–the princess Asandamitra, his wife and closest adviser. Her bright mind and grace softened even the hardest of hearts, and she didn't care for power or riches. Since childhood, she practiced *dharma*, the teachings of the Buddha on truth and compassion. Each day, she spent time in meditation and study, and she extended kindness wherever she could–to people, animals, and even tiny insects.

She easily saw past Ashoka's cold, hard manner and deep into the heart of the man who longed to be worthy of his crown.

"What good is an emperor without conquests?" Ashoka paced the throne room. It was the eighth year of his reign, and he had become increasingly agitated.

Asandamitra tried to reason with him. "Your realm is already vast," she said.

"I will expand east, to Kalinga. They have too much wealth and power to ignore! My father and grandfather could not defeat them, but I will send an army to conquer them once and for all."

And he did. But to everyone's surprise, the great Mauryan army was swiftly defeated by the determined people of Kalinga. When news of this quick defeat reached Ashoka, the old rage boiled inside him. "I will go myself and lead a much greater army. They will not stop us!" he roared.

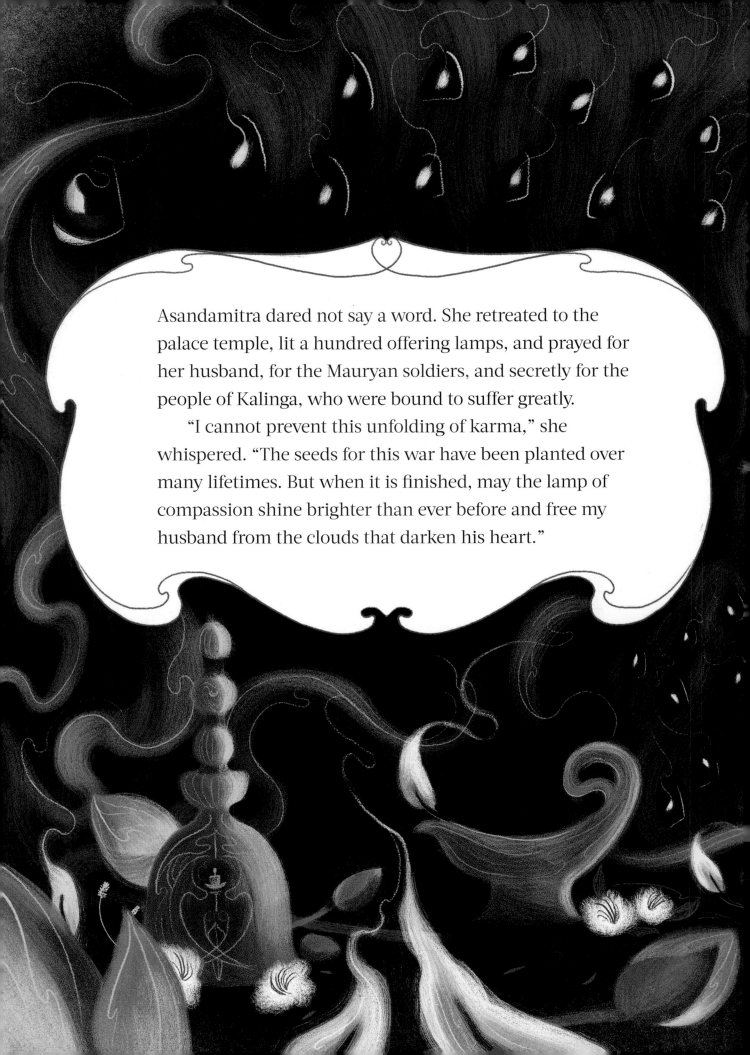

Asandamitra dared not say a word. She retreated to the palace temple, lit a hundred offering lamps, and prayed for her husband, for the Mauryan soldiers, and secretly for the people of Kalinga, who were bound to suffer greatly.

"I cannot prevent this unfolding of karma," she whispered. "The seeds for this war have been planted over many lifetimes. But when it is finished, may the lamp of compassion shine brighter than ever before and free my husband from the clouds that darken his heart."

The people of Kalinga lived peacefully on fertile land surrounded by a great forest filled with wild elephants. Rivers flowing into the bay made it a hub for trade where cultures mixed and celebrated with art, music, crafts, and spiritual study. The people were strong, proud, and ready to defend their land.

Ashoka descended with his vast army of soldiers on elephants, on horseback, in chariots, and on foot, certain of a swift and decisive victory. But the people of Kalinga roused all their resources and might. Their unwillingness to submit inflamed Ashoka's rage. As thousands of soldiers on both sides fell, he fought back ruthlessly. In the end, the people of Kalinga were no match for the force of Ashoka's army and determination.

The morning after his victory, Ashoka set out at sunrise to survey his newly won territory. The clashing metal and thundering hooves of the battlefield had given way to distant cries of people in mourning. Smoke thickened the air as thousands of homes burned to the ground. Hordes of animals squealed in fright, fleeing the blazing forest. The magnificent Daya River ran red with blood. Everywhere lay bodies from both sides of the war.

"What have I done?" Never, in all his dreams of winning, had Ashoka imagined the scene before him.

"You have achieved a great victory, Your Majesty," replied the general by his side.

Haunted by the sights and sounds of destruction, Ashoka felt his heart grow heavier and heavier as he rode home.

Asandamitra greeted him silently, her eyes full of tears.

"What have I done?" Ashoka whispered again, terrified that his gentle wife would never forgive him.

"Come." She guided him to a sunny courtyard where parrots played in the trees.

"You can't change yesterday's storm. But no matter how *fierce*"–she squeezed his hand–"every storm passes."

    "I don't want to be Ashoka the Fierce anymore."

    "Then clear the clouds in your heart and let your light shine on all your people," she said.

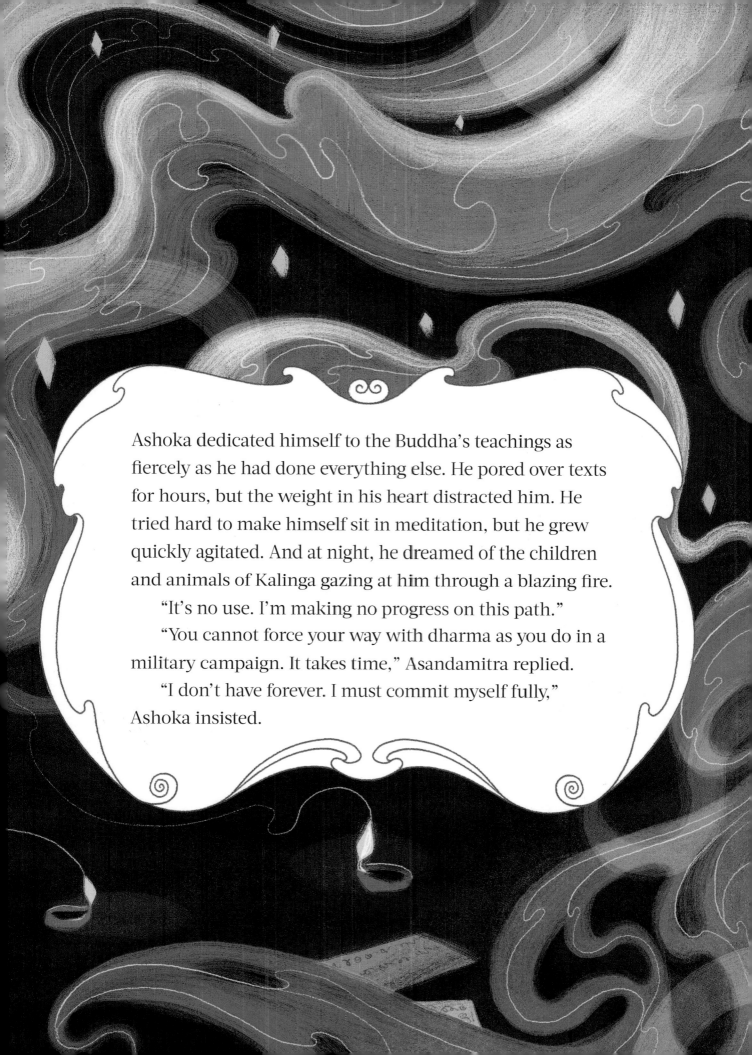

Ashoka dedicated himself to the Buddha's teachings as fiercely as he had done everything else. He pored over texts for hours, but the weight in his heart distracted him. He tried hard to make himself sit in meditation, but he grew quickly agitated. And at night, he dreamed of the children and animals of Kalinga gazing at him through a blazing fire.

"It's no use. I'm making no progress on this path."

"You cannot force your way with dharma as you do in a military campaign. It takes time," Asandamitra replied.

"I don't have forever. I must commit myself fully," Ashoka insisted.

"I will seek out the great hermit Upagupta to ordain me as a monk!" Ashoka announced impatiently.

"Your Majesty, it will not do," his minister said. "You are the emperor. He is a simple monk. *You* must summon *him*!" But Ashoka would not relent. As he prepared to make the journey to the monk's simple mountain retreat, far from the busy world, a small boat docked near the palace. Upagupta himself stepped lightly onto the shore, as if by magic.

Ashoka threw himself down at the old man's feet in gratitude, certain that now he would find the peaceful life of a monk.

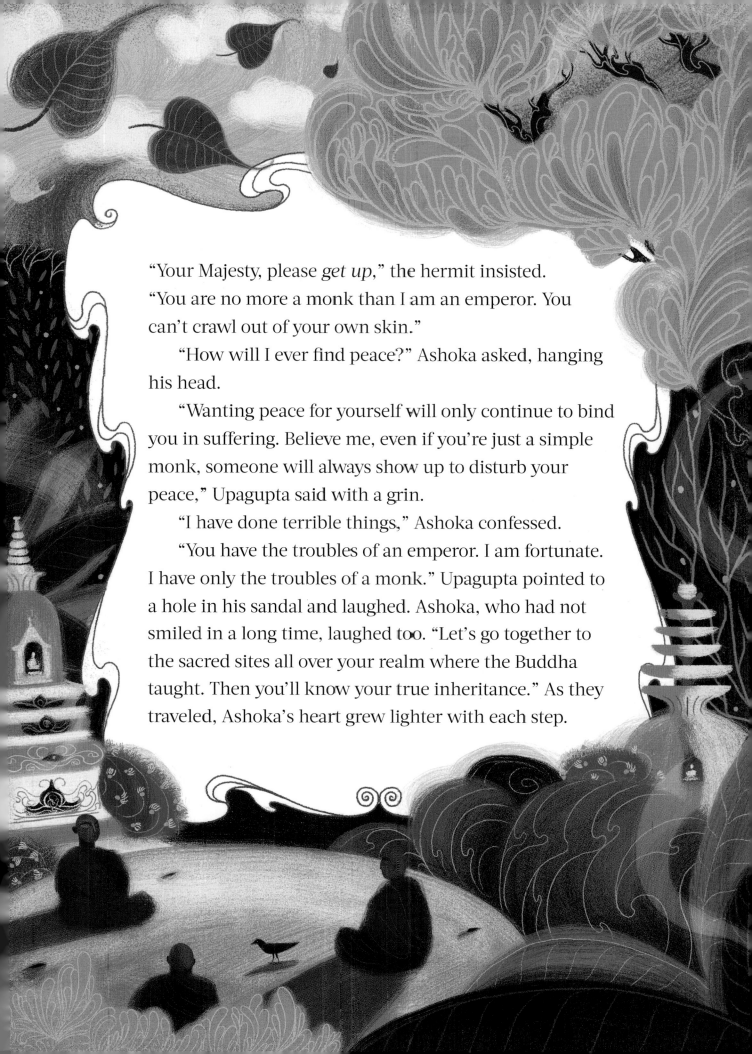

"Your Majesty, please *get up*," the hermit insisted. "You are no more a monk than I am an emperor. You can't crawl out of your own skin."

"How will I ever find peace?" Ashoka asked, hanging his head.

"Wanting peace for yourself will only continue to bind you in suffering. Believe me, even if you're just a simple monk, someone will always show up to disturb your peace," Upagupta said with a grin.

"I have done terrible things," Ashoka confessed.

"You have the troubles of an emperor. I am fortunate. I have only the troubles of a monk." Upagupta pointed to a hole in his sandal and laughed. Ashoka, who had not smiled in a long time, laughed too. "Let's go together to the sacred sites all over your realm where the Buddha taught. Then you'll know your true inheritance." As they traveled, Ashoka's heart grew lighter with each step.

Upon his return, Ashoka had transformed so radically, he began to turn everything upside down. No one knew what to expect next.

"Stop!" Ashoka shouted at a servant herding a line of animals. "Where are you taking them?"

"To slaughter for Your Majesty's celebration," the servant answered.

"There's no celebration in slaughter!" Ashoka called back. "Free them. From now on, we will eat as little meat as possible." The servant bowed nervously. "We will declare 'no killing days,' when even fishermen rest. And we'll protect the lives of monkeys and rhinos and turtles. . . ." The list went on.

Ashoka built free hospitals for people and animals, planted trees to shade weary travelers, and freed many prisoners. He trained all his officials to be kind and merciful, and attended to important matters day and night.

Ashoka gave away so much from the royal treasury, the ministers eventually barred him from accessing it. He then generously gave his personal wealth to those in need throughout his days.

"You work constantly for your people, yet still you worry," Asandamitra observed late one night after his return from a long tour of cities and villages far from the palace.

"It's not enough just to make people comfortable," Ashoka reflected. "All their suffering will continue if they cannot live together in harmony. We must encourage everyone in the way of dharma–to live honestly and with compassion for all."

"You are no longer Ashoka the Fierce." Asandamitra smiled at him. "Do you know what they call you now?

Ashoka the Great!"

Historical Note

Ashoka ruled the great Mauryan Empire from 268 to 232 B.C.E.—over 2,200 years ago. His empire encompassed all of modern-day India and extended into parts of what today are Afghanistan, Pakistan, and Iran.

Ashoka's edicts, inscribed on rocks and pillars, have been found all over the Indian subcontinent and are among the first examples of writing in Indian history. He expressed deep regret for the suffering caused by the battle at Kalinga and assured people along the borders that he had no intention of conquering further. His edicts urged everyone to care for one another, live in truth and harmony, and respect all spiritual paths.

The most famous of Ashoka's pillars stands at Sarnath, the place where the Buddha first taught. The "capital," or topmost part, of the Sarnath pillar holds a sculpture with four lions facing in each of the four directions. Their mouths are open, roaring, said to symbolize the spread of dharma in all directions. Inscribed at the top are the words SATYAMEVA JAYATE, meaning "Truth alone triumphs."

Inspired by Ashoka's vision of nonviolence, goodwill, and living in truth, India adopted the Lion Capital as its national emblem on January 26, 1950, the day India officially became a republic.

Although the Buddha taught more than two hundred years before Ashoka ascended the throne, the followers of Buddhism had remained relatively few. It was with Ashoka's reign that the teachings of the Buddha began to spread far and wide, throughout Asia and even into Greece. And yet, while Ashoka personally practiced Buddhism, he remained adamant about the importance of respecting all spiritual paths.

Above all, Ashoka gives us a powerful example of a ruler who radically changed his life to live in accord with the Buddha's teachings. Turning away from violence and the drive to conquer, he set forth an ideal of leadership driven by truthfulness, benevolence, care for the environment, and respect and compassion for all.

I see all beings as my family. My greatest
wish is for their welfare and happiness,
in this world and the next. I wish this for
them just as I do my own children.